T0057983

ALSO BY JOHN BERRYMAN

POETRY

Poems (1942)

The Dispossessed (1948)

Homage to Mistress Bradstreet (1956)

His Thought Made Pockets & The Plane Buckt (1958)

Berryman's Sonnets (1967)

Short Poems (1967)

Homage to Mistress Bradstreet and Other Poems (1968)

His Toy, His Dream, His Rest (1968)

The Dream Songs (1969)

Love & Fame (1970)

Delusions, Etc. (1972)

Henry's Fate & Other Poems, 1967–1972 (1977)

Collected Poems 1937–1971 (1989)

The Heart Is Strange (2014)

PROSE

Stephen Crane: A Critical Biography (1950)

The Arts of Reading (with Ralph Ross and Allen Tate) (1960)

Recovery (1973)

The Freedom of the Poet (1976)

Berryman's Shakespeare (1999)

77 DREAM SONGS

JOHN BERRYMAN

77 *Dream Songs*

Farrar, Straus and Giroux

New York

Farrar, Straus and Giroux
120 Broadway, New York 10271

Published in 1964 by Farrar, Straus and Giroux
This paperback edition, 2014

Library of Congress Control Number: 64014107
Paperback ISBN: 978-0-374-53452-3

Farrar, Straus and Giroux books may be purchased for educational, business, or
promotional use. For information on bulk purchases, please contact the Macmillan
Corporate and Premium Sales Department at 1-800-221-7945, extension 5442, or
write to specialmarkets@macmillan.com.

Designed by Guy Fleming

www.fsgbooks.com
www.twitter.com/fsgbooks • www.facebook.com/fsgbooks

P1

To Kate, and to Saul

"THOU DREWEST NEAR IN THE DAY"

'GO IN, BRACK MAN, DE DAY'S YO' OWN.'

. . . I AM THEIR MUSICK

Lam. 3:63

BUT THERE IS ANOTHER METHOD.

Olive Schreiner

CONTENTS

III

"DEEP IN THE MESS OF THINGS"
by Henri Cole

There is no poet who sounds like John Berryman in his 77 *Dream Songs*. He is an underground poet who made up a new kind of poem. In 1965, when he was fifty, he received the Pulitzer Prize in Poetry for this daring sequence, and just seven years later, in Minneapolis, he jumped to his death from the Washington Avenue Bridge onto the ice of the Mississippi River.

Berryman belonged to the new generation of poets emerging in the 1940s that included Robert Lowell, Sylvia Plath, Theodore Roethke, and Delmore Schwartz. Like his predecessors, he wrote skillful, intelligent poems, but he no longer felt adherent to T. S. Eliot's cult of impersonality. Instead, his poems dealt with experience often at the edge of disintegration and breakdown. In 77 *Dream Songs*, Berryman discovered a looser style that mixed high and low dictions with a strange syntax in a caudate sonnet of three six-line stanzas. His protagonist, Henry, stumbles along through life, a kind of antihero or front man, who, according to Berryman, both is and isn't him. "We touch at certain points," he explained. "But I am an actual human being; he [Henry] is nothing but a series of conceptions—my conceptions." Still, like Berryman, who suffered from alcoholism and depression, Henry is troubled, vulnerable, vehement, libidinous—and he is a white American in early middle age living at some outer boundary where the soul is in crisis. You might say that the speaker of the Dream Songs, Henry, is a modern day Saint Augustine—a writer of particular interest to Berryman—who talks about himself in the first, second, and third person. "Henry has a hard time. People don't like him, and he doesn't seem to like himself," Berryman said about Henry. Sometimes he doesn't even know his name: he's either Henry or he's Henry Pussy-cat or he's Henry House. Sometimes the poems are dialogues with an unnamed friend who calls him Mr. Bones, though Berryman would put quotation marks around *friend*, "because this is one of the most hostile friends who ever lived," who keeps questioning the author and speaking for him.

John Berryman was born John Allyn Smith, Jr., in Oklahoma in 1914, and brought up a strict Roman Catholic in the small town of Anadarko. When he was still a boy, the family moved to Tampa, Florida, where in 1926 his father, John Allyn Smith, Sr., killed himself. In her sympathetic memoir *Poets in Their Youth*, Eileen Simpson, Berryman's first wife, writes, "John had felt a compulsion to go in search of his father's ghost, a search which, though he wasn't consciously aware of it, would lead him to a new poetic subject and *The Dream Songs*." In Dream Song #42, Henry asks his dead father to remember him:

O journeyer, deaf in the mould, insane
with violent travel & death: consider me
in my cast, your first son.

Soon after being widowed, the poet's mother married a banker named John Berryman, and her son took his surname before attending boarding school in Connecticut. Later, at Columbia University, he studied with the literary scholar Mark Van Doren, who is credited with sparking Berryman's serious interest in writing poetry.

Berryman's classmate Robert Giroux was a quiet, passionate literary man who would eventually become his editor at Farrar,

Straus and Giroux; while they were still students in the 1930s, Giroux published Berryman's first poems in the college literary magazine. In an interview for *The Paris Review*, Giroux says that Berryman's mother caused her son to have difficulties greater than his illness. He calls her "a campus mother who haunted him daily, from his undergraduate days at John Jay Hall to his wintertime suicide in Minneapolis in 1972." She was so theatrical that when she phoned Giroux with the news of her son's death, instead of reporting straightaway that he'd killed himself, she said, "Bob, John has gone in under the water." Giroux didn't at first understand what she meant, but one of Berryman's suicide poems had spoken of him going in "under the water":

> Soon part of me will explore the deep and dark
> Floor of the harbour . . . I am everywhere,
> I suffer and move, my mind and my heart move
> With all that move me, under the water
> Or whistling, I am not a little boy.
> {"The Ball Poem"}

Berryman's mother (who had changed her name from Martha to Jill at the request of her new husband) believed her son had slipped from the Minneapolis bridge and that it wasn't a suicide. Forty-four years earlier, she hadn't believed her husband's death was a suicide either, though he'd shot himself in the chest outside their son's bedroom window. She told her son that she'd removed all the bullets from the gun, which she'd kept around only "to frighten any thieves or rascals away." All his life, Berryman felt guilt-ridden about his father's death at the age of thirty-nine, and his poems often revisit the violent facts.

In his own interview for *The Paris Review*, Berryman explains that the Dream Songs are not "confessional poems." He understands the confessional "to be a place where you go and talk with a priest," and he hasn't been to confession since he was twelve years old. He sees himself as an epic poet and the collected Dream Songs are a long poem—with the greatest American poem, Walt Whitman's "Song of Myself," as his model. It too has a hero, a personality, and a self, but Berryman doesn't think his poem goes as far as Whitman's. He calls "Song of Myself" a "wisdom work" about "the meaning of life and how to conduct it," but according to him, *"The Dream Songs* does not propose a new system; that is not the point."

If in poetry the first person pronoun—the "I"—is not the poet, it is even less so in a Berryman Dream Song, where the speaker modulates immediately into Henry. And when it comes to Henry's religious and political opinions, they might not even be Henry's, since the poems are a transcript of his tragicomic nightmares. And since there is no structured plot to 77 *Dream Songs*, it coheres as a work about the personality of Henry rather than as a continuous narrative. According to Berryman, all the way through his poetry there

> is a tendency to regard the individual soul under stress. The soul is not oneself, for the personal 'I', one with a social security number and a bank account, never gets into the poems; they are all about a third person. I'm a follower of Pascal in the sense that I don't know what the issue is, or how it is to be resolved—the issue of our common human life, yours, mine, your lady's, everybody's; but I do think that one way in which we can approach it, by the means of art, coming out of Homer and Virgil and down through

Yeats and Eliot, is by investigating the individual human soul, or human mind.

Berryman believed that writing poems was a vocation that demanded the attention of his whole being. His friend Saul Bellow said that he drew his writing "out of his vital organs, out of his very skin." He spent thirteen years writing the Dream Songs and in them rejects the decorous Anglophilia and formal versification that were fashionable during the previous decade. "I set up *The Dream Songs* as hostile to every visible tendency in both American and English poetry," Berryman said. Instead, we get a new kind of diction—ridiculous, grotesque, horrible, delicious—that better suits the generally extravagant situations in which the sobbing protagonist Henry finds himself.

At a public reading, Robert Lowell described Berryman's poems as being of a sort that people didn't expect to see again. They are obscure, and they revive obscurity at a time when people thought it was finished (though this assessment ignores a countertradition in American poetry that includes Black Mountain, the New York School, and the San Francisco Renaissance poets). "A lot of the best poetry of the century is extremely difficult," Lowell tells his audience, and he doesn't mean "such poems as 'The Waste Land,' which originally seemed difficult and is now simpler than Longfellow almost." According to him, there are certain poems that remain difficult—like the "Atlantis" section of Hart Crane's *The Bridge*—and great. After the Modern poets—Stevens, Eliot, Ransom, Moore, Crane, Pound, and Frost—suddenly poetry was clear again, Lowell says. People felt you couldn't be unintelligible anymore. But then Berryman's poems began to appear, and "they made all the clear stuff seem mannered and tired."

Berryman and Lowell met at Princeton in 1944, during the waning of the war, and Lowell found Berryman to have "a casual intensity" and the "almost intimate mumble of a don." He loved Hopkins, Yeats, and Auden, whose "shadows paled him." "Berryman might have grown into an austere, removed poet," Lowell felt, "but instead he somehow remained deep in the mess of things. His writing has been a long, often back-breaking search for an inclusive style, a style that could use his erudition and catch the high, even frenetic, intensity of his experience, disgusts, and enthusiasms." The Dream Songs, with their "racy jabber," are "larger and sloppier" than anything Berryman had written before. Writing in *The New York Review of Books*, Lowell described their bruised world of "remorse, wonder, and nightmare":

> The scene is contemporary and crowded with references to news items, world politics, travel, low life, and Negro music. Its style is a conglomeration of high style, Berryman-isms, Negro and beat slang, and baby talk...There is little sequence, and sometimes a single section will explode into three or four separate parts. At first the brain aches and freezes at so much darkness, disorder, and oddness...The poems are much too difficult, packed, and wrenched to be sung. They are called *songs* out of mockery, because they are filled with snatches of Negro minstrelsy...The dreams are not real dreams but a waking hallucination in which anything that might have happened to the author can be used at random. Anything he has seen, overheard, or imagined can go in. The poems are Berryman, or rather they are about a person he calls *Henry*. Henry is Berryman seen as himself, as *poète maudit*, child and puppet. He is tossed about with a mixture of tenderness and absurdity, pathos

and hilarity that would have been impossible if the author had spoken in the first person.

In a letter to his friend Elizabeth Bishop, Lowell calls 77 *Dream Songs* "spooky, a maddening work of genius, or half genius, in John's later obscure, tortured, wandering style, full of parentheses, slang no one ever spoke, jagged haunting lyrical moments, etc." And Bishop replies, "I'm pretty much at sea about that book—some pages I find wonderful, some baffle me completely. I am sure he is saying *something* important—perhaps sometimes too personally?" Elsewhere, she praises the "wonderful little things, in flashes—the glitter of broken glasses, smashed museum cases—something like that."

Before Berryman published 77 *Dream Songs*, his historical poem "Homage to Mistress Bradstreet" had been called "the most distinguished long poem by an American since 'The Waste Land.'" It was one of the famous academic poems of the 1950s, though today it is largely eclipsed by the more original, less shapely, occasionally volcanic, continually haranguing 77 *Dream Songs*, with its wild syntax that suggests a heavy heart and a frightened, self-pitying, angry, guilty, irritable, and generally aberrant mind. After the Bradstreet poem was published, there was a silence of two years before Berryman began writing the Dream Songs, which he continued working on until his death.

The Dream Songs is a work consisting of 385 individual poems compiled in two books, 77 *Dreams Songs* (1964), which makes up its first part, and *His Toy, His Dream, His Rest* (1968). In a note for the second book, Berryman writes that it "continues and concludes" the poem called *The Dream Songs*. Speaking in general about long poems, he says, "Both the writer and the reader of long poems need gall, the outrageous, the intolerable—and they need it again and again. The prospect of ignominious failure must haunt them continually. Whitman, our greatest poet, had all this. Eliot, next, perhaps even greater than Whitman, had it too. Pound makes a marvelous if frail third here." Further complicating the publication history of *The Dream Songs*, a third book, *Henry's Fate and Other Poems*, appeared posthumously, containing forty-five unpublished or uncollected Dream Songs.

Among the best poems in 77 *Dream Songs* (#1, #4, #5, #14, #21, #26, #29, #37, #45, #46, #53, #76, and #77) are many lines that have entered American poetry's consciousness:

Once in a sycamore I was glad
all at the top, and I sang.
[#1]

Filling her compact & delicious body
with chicken páprika, she glanced at me
twice.
[#4]

Life, friends, is boring. We must not say so.
[#14]

—I had a most marvelous   piece of luck. I died.
[#26]

There sat down, once, a thing on Henry's heart
só heavy, if he had a hundred years
& more, & weeping, sleepless, in all them time
Henry could not make good.
[#29]

He stared at ruin. Ruin stared straight back.
[#45]

Nothin very bad happen to me lately.
[#76]

Why write poems? I sometimes wonder, as Berryman did. The list of reasons is long: despair, pleasure, insomnia, selfishness, sublimation, habit, boredom, anger, jealousy, disappointment, sorrow, self-pity, self-reform, self-delusion, hunger—for praise and prestige and posterity. But also for health. Despite a diagnosis of a cyclothymic personality (a bipolar disorder) and habitual excessive drinking, despite insomnia and frightening dreams, and despite a "severely grossly tremulous" existence, Berryman somehow found a way to assemble language into art that—in a psychiatric form—represented his world and himself. 77 *Dream Songs*, with its agonizing, volatile, obsessive, distorted temperamental boldness, is a triumph against his ordeal. And as Berryman himself put it, with characteristic black humor, "I do strongly feel that among the greatest pieces of luck for high achievement is ordeal . . . The artist is extremely lucky who is presented with the worst possible ordeal which will not actually kill him. At that point, he's in business."

AUTHOR'S NOTE

These are sections, constituting one version, of a poem in progress. Its working title, since 1955, has been *The Dream Songs*. One is dedicated (2) to the memory of Daddy Rice who sang and jumped 'Jim Crow' in Louisville in 1828 (London, 1836 and later), and others to friends: Robert Giroux (7), John Crowe Ransom (*11*), Howard Munford (*24*), Ralph Ross (27), Robert Fitzgerald (*34*), Daniel Hughes (*35*), William Meredith (*36*), the Theodore Morrisons and the Chisholm Gentrys (*37–38–39*), Dr A. Boyd Thomes (54), Edmund and Elena Wilson (*58*), George Amberg (*63*), Mark Van Doren (*66*), Allen and Isabella Tate (*70*), Saul Bellow (*75*). The editors directing certain journals have been hospitable to some of the Songs here brought together: *The Times Literary Supplement, The Noble Savage, The Observer, Poetry, Partisan Review, Encounter, Poetry Northwest, The New York Review of Books, The New Republic, Minnesota Review, Harpers, Ramparts, The Yale Review, The Kenyon Review.* Many opinions and errors in the Songs are to be referred not to the character Henry, still less to the author, but to the title of the work.

J.B.

I

1

Huffy Henry hid   the day,
unappeasable Henry sulked.
I see his point,—a trying to put things over.
It was the thought that they thought
they could *do* it made Henry wicked & away.
But he should have come out and talked.

All the world like a woolen lover
once did seem on Henry's side.
Then came a departure.
Thereafter nothing fell out as it might or ought.
I don't see how Henry, pried
open for all the world to see, survived.

What he has now to say is a long
wonder the world can bear & be.
Once in a sycamore I was glad
all at the top, and I sang.
Hard on the land wears the strong sea
and empty grows every bed.

2

Big Buttons, Cornets: the advance

The jane is zoned! no nightspot here, no bar
there, no sweet freeway, and no premises
for business purposes,
no loiterers or needers. Henry are
baffled. Have ev'ybody head for Maine,
utility-man take a train?

Arrive a time when all coons lose dere grip,
but is he come? Le's do a hoedown, gal,
one blue, one shuffle,
if them is all you seem to réquire. Strip,
ol banger, skip us we, sugar; so hang on
one chaste evenin.

—Sir Bones, or Galahad: astonishin
yo legal & yo good. Is you feel well?
Honey dusk do sprawl.
—Hit's hard. Kinged or thinged, though, fling & wing.
Poll-cats are coming, hurrah, hurray.
I votes in my hole.

3

A Stimulant for an Old Beast

Acacia, burnt myrrh, velvet, pricky stings.
—I'm not so young but not so very old,
said screwed-up lovely 23.
A final sense of being right out in the cold,
unkissed.
(—My psychiatrist can lick your psychiatrist.) Women get under
   things.

All these old criminals sooner or later
have had it. I've been reading old journals.
Gottwald & Co., out of business now.
Thick chests quit. Double agent, Joe.
She holds her breath like a seal
and is whiter & smoother.

Rilke was a *jerk*.
I admit his griefs & music
& titled spelled all-disappointed ladies.
A threshold worse than the circles
where the vile settle & lurk,
Rilke's. As I said,—

4

Filling her compact & delicious body
with chicken páprika, she glanced at me
twice.
Fainting with interest, I hungered back
and only the fact of her husband & four other people
kept me from springing on her

or falling at her little feet and crying
'You are the hottest one for years of night
Henry's dazed eyes
have enjoyed, Brilliance.' I advanced upon
(despairing) my spumoni. —Sir Bones: is stuffed,
de world, wif feeding girls.

—Black hair, complexion Latin, jewelled eyes
downcast . . . The slob beside her   feasts . . . What wonders is
she sitting on, over there?
The restaurant buzzes. She might as well be on Mars.
Where did it all go wrong? There ought to be a law against Henry.
—Mr. Bones: there is.

Henry sats in de bar & was odd,
off in the glass from the glass,
at odds wif de world & its god,
his wife is a complete nothing,
St Stephen
getting even.

Henry sats in de plane & was gay.
Careful Henry nothing said aloud
but where a Virgin out of cloud
to her Mountain dropt in light,
his thought made pockets & the plane buckt.
'Parm me, lady.' 'Orright.'

Henry lay in de netting, wild,
while the brainfever bird did scales;
Mr Heartbreak, the New Man,
come to farm a crazy land;
an image of the dead on the fingernail
of a newborn child.

6

A Capital at Wells

During the father's walking—how he look
down by now in soft boards, Henry, pass
and what he feel or no, who know?—
as during hís broad father's, all the breaks
& ill-lucks of a thriving pioneer
back to the flying boy in mountain air,

Vermont's child to go out, and while Keats sweat'
for hopeless inextricable lust, Henry's fate,
and Ethan Allen was a calling man,
all through the blind one's dream of the start,
when Day was killing Porter and had to part
lovers for ever, fancy if you can,

while the cardinals' guile to keep Aeneas out
was failing, while in some hearts Chinese doubt
inscrutably was growing, toward its end,
and a starved lion by a water-hole
clouded with gall, while Abelard was whole,
these grapes of stone were being proffered, friend.

'The Prisoner of Shark Island'
with Paul Muni

Henry is old, old; for Henry remembers
Mr Deeds' tuba, & the Cameo,
& the race in *Ben Hur*,—*The Lost World*, with sound,
& *The Man from Blankley's*, which he did not dig,
nor did he understand one caption of,
bewildered Henry, while the Big Ones laughed.

Now Henry is unmistakably a Big One.
Fúnnee; he don't féel so.
He just stuck around.
The German & the Russian films into
Italian & Japanese films turned, while many
were prevented from making it.

He wishing he could squirm again where Hoot
is just ahead of rustlers, where William S
forgoes some deep advantage, & moves on,
where Hashknife Hartley having the matter taped
the rats are flying. For the rats
have moved in, mostly, and this is for real.

9

The weather was fine. They took away his teeth,
white & helpful; bothered his backhand;
halved his green hair.
They blew out his loves, his interests. 'Underneath,'
(they called in iron voices) 'understand,
is nothing. So there.'

The weather was very fine. They lifted off
his covers till he showed, and cringed & pled
to see himself less.
They installed mirrors till he flowed. 'Enough'
(murmured they) 'if you will watch Us instead,
yet you may saved be. Yes.'

The weather fleured. They weakened all his eyes,
and burning thumbs into his ears, and shook
his hand like a notch.
They flung long silent speeches. (Off the hook!)
They sandpapered his plumpest hope. (So capsize.)
They took away his crotch.

Deprived of his enemy, shrugged to a standstill
horrible Henry, foaming. Fan their way
toward him who will
in the high wood: the officers, their rest,
with p. a. echoing: his girl comes, say,
conned in to test

if he's still human, see: she love him, see,
therefore she get on the Sheriff's mike & howl
'Come down, come down'.
Therefore he un-budge, furious. He'd flee
but only Heaven hangs over him foul.
At the crossways, downtown,

he dreams the folks are buying parsnips & suds
and paying rent to foes. He slipt & fell.
It's golden here in the snow.
A mild crack: a far rifle. Bogart's duds
truck back to Wardrobe. Fancy the brain from hell
held out so long. Let go.

1 0

There were strange gatherings. A vote would come
that would be no vote. There would come a rope.
Yes. There would come a rope.
Men have their hats down. "Dancing in the Dark"
will see him up, car-radio-wise. So many, some
won't find a rut to park.

It is in the administration of rhetoric,
on these occasions, that—not the fathomless heart—
the thinky death consists;
his chest is pinched. The enemy are sick,
and so is us of. Often, to rising trysts,
like this one, drove he out

and the gasps of love, after all, had got him ready.
However things hurt, men hurt worse. He's stark
to be jerked onward?
Yes. In the headlights he got' keep him steady,
leak not, look out over. This' hard work,
boss, wait' for The Word.

His mother goes. The mother comes & goes.
Chen Lung's too came, came and crampt & then
that dragoner's mother was gone.
It seem we don't have no good bed to lie on,
forever. While he drawing his first breath,
while skinning his knees,

while he was so beastly with love for Charlotte Coquet
he skated up & down in front of her house
wishing he could, sir, die,
while being bullied & he dreamt he could fly—
during irregular verbs—them world-sought bodies
safe in the Arctic lay:

Strindberg rocked in his niche, the great Andrée
by muscled Fraenkel under what's of the tent,
torn like then limbs, by bears
over fierce decades, harmless. Up in pairs
go we not, but we have a good bed.
I have said what I had to say.

Sabbath

There is an eye, there was a slit.
Nights walk, and confer on him fear.
The strangler tree, the dancing mouse
confound his vision; then they loosen it.
Henry widens. How did Henry House
himself ever come here?

Nights run. Tes yeux bizarres me suivent
when loth at landfall soft I leave.
The soldiers, Coleridge Rilke Poe,
shout commands I never heard.
They march about, dying & absurd.
Toddlers are taking over. O

ver! Sabbath belling. Snoods converge
on a weary-daring man.
What now can be cleared up? from the Yard the visitors urge.
Belle thro' the graves in a blast of sun
to the kirk moves the youngest witch.
Watch.

13

God bless Henry. He lived like a rat,
with a thatch of hair on his head
in the beginning.
Henry was not a coward. Much.
He never deserted anything; instead
he stuck, when things like pity were thinning.

So may be Henry was a human being.
Let's investigate that.
. . . We did; okay.
He is a human American man.
That's true. My lass is braking.
My brass is aching. Come & diminish me, & map my way.

God's Henry's enemy. We're in business . . . Why,
what business must be clear.
A cornering.
I couldn't feel more like it. —Mr Bones,
as I look on the saffron sky,
you strikes me as ornery.

Life, friends, is boring. We must not say so.
After all, the sky flashes, the great sea yearns,
we ourselves flash and yearn,
and moreover my mother told me as a boy
(repeatingly) 'Ever to confess you're bored
means you have no

Inner Resources.' I conclude now I have no
inner resources, because I am heavy bored.
Peoples bore me,
literature bores me, especially great literature,
Henry bores me, with his plights & gripes
as bad as achilles,

who loves people and valiant art, which bores me.
And the tranquil hills, & gin, look like a drag
and somehow a dog
has taken itself & its tail considerably away
into mountains or sea or sky, leaving
behind: me, wag.

Let us suppose, valleys & such ago,
one pal unwinding from his labours in
one bar of Chicago,
and this did actual happen. This was so.
And many graces are slipped, & many a sin
even that laid man low

but this will be remembered & told over,
that she was heard at last, haughtful & greasy,
to bawl in that low bar:
'You can biff me, you can bang me, get it you'll never.
I may be only a Polack   broad but I don't lay easy.
Kiss my ass, that's what you are.'

Women is better, braver. In a foehn of loss
entire, which too they hotter understand,
having had it,
we struggle. Some hang heavy on the sauce,
some invest in the past, one hides in the land.
Henry was not his favourite.

Henry's pelt was put on sundry walls
where it did much resemble Henry and
them persons was delighted.
Especially his long & glowing tail
by all them was admired, and visitors.
They whistled: This is *it*!

Golden, whilst your frozen daiquiris
whir at midnight, gleams on you his fur
& silky & black.
Mission accomplished, pal.
My molten yellow & moonless bag,
drained, hangs at rest.

Collect in the cold depths barracuda. Ay,
in Sealdah Station some possessionless
children survive to die.
The Chinese communes hum. Two daiquiris
withdrew into a corner of the gorgeous room
and one told the other a lie.

Muttered Henry:—Lord of matter, thus:
upon some more unquiet spirit knock,
my madnesses have cease.
All the quarter astonishes a lonely out & back.
They set their clocks by Henry House,
the steadiest man on the block.

And Lucifer:—I smell you for my own,
by smug. —What have I tossed you but the least
(tho' hard); fit for your ears.
Your servant, bored with horror, sat alone
with busy teeth while his dislike increased
unto himself, in tears.

And he:—O promising despair,
in solitude— —End there.
Your avenues are dying: leave me: I dove
under the oaken arms of Brother Martin,
St Simeon the Lesser Theologian,
Bodhidharma, and the Baal Shem Tov.

18

A Strut for Roethke

Westward, hit a low note, for a roarer lost
across the Sound but north from Bremerton,
hit a way down note.
And never cadenza again of flowers, or cost.
Him who could really do that cleared his throat
& staggered on.

The bluebells, pool-shallows, saluted his over-needs,
while the clouds growled, heh-heh, & snapped, & crashed.

No stunt he'll ever unflinch once more will fail
(O lucky fellow, eh Bones?)—drifted off upstairs,
downstairs, somewheres.
No more daily, trying to hit the head on the nail:
thirstless: without a think in his head:
back from wherever, with it said.

Hit a high long note, for a lover found
needing a lower into friendlier ground
to bug among worms no more
around um jungles where ah blurt 'What for?'
Weeds, too, he favoured as   most men don't favour men.
The Garden Master's gone.

1 9

Here, whence
all have departed or will do, here airless, where
that witchy ball
wanted, fought toward, dreamed of, all a green living
drops limply into one's hands
without pleasure or interest

Figurez-vous, a time swarms when the word
'happy' sheds its whole meaning, like to come and
like for memory too
That morning arrived to Henry as well a great cheque
eaten out already by the Government & State &
other strange matters

Gentle friendly Henry Pussy-cat
smiled into his mirror, a murderer's
(at Stillwater), at himself alone
and said across a plink to that desolate fellow
said a little hail & buck-you-up
upon his triumph

2 0

The Secret of the Wisdom

When worst got things, how was you? Steady on?
Wheedling, or shockt her &
you have been bad to your friend,
whom not you writing to. You have not listened.
A pelican of lies
you loosed: where are you?

Down weeks of evenings of longing
by hours, NOW, a stoned bell,
you did somebody: others you hurt short:
anyone ever did you do good?
You licking your own old hurt,
what?

An evil kneel & adore.
This is human. Hurl, God who found
us in this, down
something . . . We hear the more
sin has increast, the more
grace has been caused to abound.

Some good people, daring & subtle voices
and their tense faces, as I think of it
I see sank underground.
I see. My radar digs. I do not dig.
Cool their flushing blood, them eyes is shut—
eyes?

Appalled: by all the dead: Henry brooded.
Without exception! All.
ALL.
The senior population   waits. Come down! come down!
A ghastly & flashing pause, clothed,
life called; us do.

In a madhouse heard I an ancient man
tube-fed who had not said for fifteen years
(they said) one canny word,
senile forever, who a heart might pierce,
mutter 'O come on down. O come on down.'
Clear whom *he* meant.

Of 1826

I am the little man who smokes & smokes.
I am the girl who does know better but.
I am the king of the pool.
I am so wise I had my mouth sewn shut.
I am a government official & a goddamned fool.
I am a lady who takes jokes.

I am the enemy of the mind.
I am the auto salesman and lóve you.
I am a teenage cancer, with a plan.
I am the blackt-out man.
I am the woman powerful as a zoo.
I am two eyes screwed to my set, whose blind—

It is the Fourth of July.
Collect: while the dying man,
forgone by you creator, who forgives,
is gasping 'Thomas Jefferson still lives'
in vain, in vain, in vain.
I am Henry Pussy-cat! My whiskers fly.

2 3

The Lay of Ike

This is the lay of Ike.
Here's to the glory of the Great White—awk—
who has been running—er—er—things in recent—ech—
in the United—If your screen is black,
ladies & gentlemen, we—I like—
at the Point he was already terrific—sick

to a second term, having done no wrong—
no right—no right—having let the Army—bang—
defend itself from Joe, let venom' Strauss
bile Oppenheimer out of use—use Robb,
who'll later fend for Goldfine—Breaking no laws,
he lay in the White House—sob!!—

who never understood his own strategy—whee—
so Monty's memoirs—nor any strategy,
wanting the ball bulled thro' all parts of the line
at once—proving, by his refusal to take Berlin,
he misread even Clauswitz—wide empty grin
that never lost a vote (O Adlai mine).

Oh servant Henry lectured till
the crows commenced and then
he bulbed his voice & lectured on some more.
This happened again & again, like war,—
the Indian p.a.'s, such as they were,
a weapon on his side, for the birds.

Vexations held a field-monsoon.
He was Introduced, and then he was Summed-up.
He was put questions on race bigotry;
he put no questions on race bigotry
constantly.
The mad sun rose though on the ghats
  & the saddhu in maha mudra, the great River,

and Henry was happy & beside him with excitement.
Beside himself, his possibilities;
salaaming hours of a half-blind morning
while the rainy lepers salaamed back,
smiles & a passion of their & his eyes flew
in feelings not ever accorded solely to oneself.

Henry, edged, decidedly, made up stories
lighting the past of Henry, of his glorious
present, and his hoaries,
all the bight heals he tamped— —Euphoria,
Mr Bones, euphoria. Fate clobber all.
—Hand me back my crawl,

condign Heaven. Tighten into a ball
elongate & valved Henry. Tuck him peace.
Render him sightless,
or ruin at high rate his crampon focus,
wipe out his need. Reduce him to the rest of us.
—But, Bones, you is that.

—I cannot remember. I am going away.
There was something in my dream about a Cat,
which fought and sang.
Something about a lyre, an island. Unstrung.
Linked to the land at low tide. Cables fray.
Thank you for everything.

The glories of the world struck me, made me aria, once.
—What happen then, Mr Bones?
if be you cares to say.
—Henry. Henry became interested in women's bodies,
his loins were & were the   scene of stupendous achievement.
Stupor. Knees, dear. Pray.

All the knobs & softnesses of, my God,
the ducking & trouble it swarm on Henry,
at one time.
—What happen then, Mr Bones?
you seems excited-like.
—Fell Henry back into   the original crime: art, rime

besides a sense of others, my God, my God,
and a jealousy for the honour (alive) of his country,
what can get more odd?
and discontent with the thriving gangs & pride.
—What happen then, Mr Bones?
—I had a most marvellous   piece of luck. I died.

II

The greens of the Ganges delta foliate.
Of heartless youth made late aware he pled:
Brownies, please come.
To Henry in his sparest times sometimes
the little people spread, & did friendly things;
then he was glad.

Pleased, at the worst, except with man, he shook
the brightest winter sun.
All the green lives
of the great delta, hours, hurt his migrant heart
in a safety of the steady 'plane. Please, please
come.

My friends,—he has been known to mourn,—I'll die;
live you, in the most wild, kindly, green
partly forgiving wood,
sort of forever and all those human sings
close not your better ears to, while good Spring
returns with a dance and a sigh.

Snow Line

It was wet & white & swift and where I am
we don't know. It was dark and then
it isn't.
I wish the barker would come. There seems to be to eat
nothing. I am unusually tired.
I'm alone too.

If only the strange one with so few legs would come,
I'd say my prayers out of my mouth, as usual.
Where are his notes I loved?
There may be horribles; it's hard to tell.
The barker nips me but somehow I feel
he too is on my side.

I'm too alone. I see no end. If we could all
run, even that would be better. I am hungry.
The sun is not hot.
It's not a good position I am in.
If I had to do the whole thing over again
I wouldn't.

There sat down, once, a thing on Henry's heart
só heavy, if he had a hundred years
& more, & weeping, sleepless, in all them time
Henry could not make good.
Starts again always in Henry's ears
the little cough somewhere, an odour, a chime.

And there is another thing he has in mind
like a grave Sienese face a thousand years
would fail to blur the still profiled reproach of. Ghastly,
with open eyes, he attends, blind.
All the bells say: too late. This is not for tears;
thinking.

But never did Henry, as he thought he did,
end anyone and hacks her body up
and hide the pieces, where they may be found.
He knows: he went over everyone, & nobody's missing.
Often he reckons, in the dawn, them up.
Nobody is ever missing.

3 0

Collating bones: I would have liked to do.
Henry would have been hot at that.
I missed his profession.
As a little boy I always thought
'I'm an archeologist'; who
could be more respected peaceful serious than that?

Hell talkt my brain awake.
Bluffed to the ends of me pain
& I took up a pencil;
like this I'm longing with. One sign
would snow me back, back.
Is there anyone in the audience who has lived in vain?

A Chinese tooth! African jaw!
Drool, says a nervous system,
for a joyous replacing. Heat burns off dew.
Between the Ices (Mindel-Würm)
in a world I ever saw
some of my dying people indexed: "Warm."

3 1

Henry Hankovitch, con guítar,
did a short Zen pray,
on his tatami in a relaxed lotos
fixin his mind on nuffin, rose-blue breasts,
and gave his parnel one French kiss;
enslaving himself he withdrew from his blue

Florentine leather case an Egyptian black
& flickt a zippo.
Henry & Phoebe happy as cockroaches
in the world-kitchen woofed, with all away.
The international flame, like despair, rose
or like the foolish Paks or Sudanese

Henry Hankovitch, con guítar,
did a praying mantis pray
who even more obviously than the increasingly fanatical Americans
cannot govern themselves. Swedes don't exist,
Scandinavians in general do not exist,
take it from there.

And where, friend Quo, lay you hiding
across malignant half my years or so?
One evil faery
it was workt night, with amoroso pleasing
menace, the panes shake
where Lie-by-the-fire is waiting for his cream.

A tiger by a torrent in rain, wind,
narrows fiend's eyes for grief
in an old ink-on-silk,
reminding me of Delphi, and,
friend Quo, once was safe
imagination as sweet milk.

Let all flowers wither like a party.
And now you have abandoned
own your young & old, the oldest, people
to a solitudinem of mournful communes,
mournful communes.
Status, Status, come home.

An apple arc'd toward Kleitos; whose great King
wroth & of wine did study where his sword,
sneaked away, might be . . .
with swollen lids staggered up and clung
dim to the cloth of gold. An un-Greek word
blister, to him his guard,

and the trumpeter would not sound, fisted. Ha,
they hustle Clitus out; by another door,
loaded, crowds he back in
who now must, chopped, fall to the spear-ax ah
grabbed from an extra by the boy-god, sore
for weapons. For the sin:

little it is gross Henry has to say.
The King heaved. Pluckt out, the ax-end would
he jab in his sole throat.
As if an end. A baby, the guard may
squire him to his apartments. Weeping & blood
wound round his one friend.

My mother has your shotgun. One man, wide
in the mind, and tendoned like a grizzly, pried
to his trigger-digit, pal.
He should not have done that, but, I guess,
he didn't feel the best, Sister,—felt less
and more about less than us . . . ?

Now—tell me, my love, *if* you recall
the dove light after dawn at the island and all—
here is the story, Jack:
he verbed for forty years, very enough,
& shot & buckt—and, baby, there was of
schist but small there (some).

Why should I tell a truth? when in the crack
of the dooming & emptying news I did hold back—
in the taxi too, sick—
silent—it's so I broke down here, in his mind
whose sire as mine one same way— I refuse,
hoping the guy go home.

MLA

Hey, out there!—assistant professors, full,
associates,—instructors—others—any—
I have a sing to shay.
We are assembled here in the capital
city for Dull—and one professor's wife is Mary—
at Christmastide, hey!

and all of you did theses or are doing
and the moral history of what we were up to
thrives in Sir Wilson's hands—
who I don't see here—only deals go screwing
some of you out, some up—the chairmen too
are nervous, little friends—

a chairman's not a chairman, son, forever,
and hurts with his appointments; ha, but circle—
take my word for it—
though maybe Frost is dying—around Mary;
forget your footnotes on the old gentleman;
dance around Mary.

3 6

The high ones die, die. They die. You look up and who's there?
—Easy, easy, Mr Bones. I is on your side.
I smell your grief.
—I sent my grief away. I cannot care
forever. With them all again & again I died
and cried, and I have to live.

—Now there *you* exaggerate, Sah. We hafta *die.*
That is our 'pointed task. Love & die.
—Yes; that makes sense.
But what makes sense between, then? What if I
roiling & babbling & braining, brood on why and
just sat on the fence?

—I doubts you did or do. De choice is lost.
—It's fool's gold. But I go in for that.
The boy & the bear
looked at each other. Man all is tossed
& lost with groin-wounds by the grand bulls, cat.
William Faulkner's where?

(Frost being still around.)

40

Three around the Old Gentleman

His malice was a pimple down his good
big face, with its sly eyes. I must be sorry
Mr Frost has left:
I like it so less I don't understood—
he couldn't hear or see well—all we sift—
but this is a *bad* story.

He had fine stories and was another man
in private; difficult, always. Courteous,
on the whole, in private.
He apologize to Henry, off & on,
for two blue slanders; which was good of him.
I don't know how he made it.

Quickly, off stage with all but kindness, now.
I can't say what I have in mind. Bless Frost,
any odd god around.
Gentle his shift, I decussate & command,
stoic deity. For a while here we possessed
an unusual man.

38

The Russian grin bellows his condolence
tó the family: ah but it's Kay,
& Ted, & Chis & Anne,
Henry thinks of: who eased his fearful way
from here, in here, to there. This wants thought.
I won't make it out.

Maybe the source of noble such may come
clearer to dazzled Henry. It may come.
I'd say it will come with pain,
in mystery. I'd rather leave it alone.
I do leave it alone.
And down with the listener.

Now he has become, abrupt, an industry.
Professional-Friends-Of-Robert-Frost all over
gap wide their mouths
while the quirky medium of so many truths
is quiet. Let's be quiet. Let us listen:
—What for, Mr Bones?
                    —while he begins to have it out with Horace.

39

Goodbye, sir, & fare well. You're in the clear.
'Nobody' (Mark says   you said) 'is ever found out.'
I figure you were right,
having as Henry got away with murder
for long. Some jarred clock tell me it's late,
not for you who went straight

but for the lorn. Our roof is lefted off
lately: the shooter, and the bourbon man,
and then you got tired.
I'm afraid that's it. I figure you with love,
lifey, deathy, but I have a little sense
the rest of us are fired

or fired: be with us: we will blow our best,
our sad wild riffs come easy in that case,
thinking you over,
knowing you resting, who was reborn to rest,
your gorgeous sentence done. Nothing's the same,
sir,—taking cover.

4 0

I'm scared a lonely. Never see my son,
easy be not to see anyone,
combers out to sea
know they're goin somewhere but not me.
Got a little poison, got a little gun,
I'm scared a lonely.

I'm scared a only one thing, which is me,
from othering I don't take nothin, see,
for any hound dog's sake.
But this is where I livin, where I rake
my leaves and cop my promise, this' where we
cry oursel's awake.

Wishin was dyin but I gotta make
it all this way to that bed on these feet
where peoples said to meet.
Maybe but even if I see my son
forever never, get back on the take,
free, black & forty-one.

4 1

If we sang in the wood (and Death is a German expert)
while snows flies, chill, after so frequent knew
so many all of nothing,
for lead & fire, it's not we would assert
particulars, but animal; cats mew,
horses scream, man sing.

Or: men psalm. Man palms his ears and moans.
Death is a German expert. Scrambling, sitting,
spattering, we hurry.
I try to. Odd & trivial, atones
somehow for *my* escape a bullet splitting
my trod-on instep, fiery.

The cantor bubbled, rattled. The Temple burned.
Lurch with me! phantoms of Varshava. Slop!
When I used to be,
who haunted, stumbling, sewers, my sacked shop,
roofs, a dis-world *ai!* Death was a German
home-country.

O journeyer, deaf in the mould, insane
with violent travel & death: consider me
in my cast, your first son.
Would you were I by now another one,
witted, legged? I see you before me plain
(I am skilled: I hear, I see)—

your honour was troubled: when you wondered—'No'.
I hear. I think I hear. Now full craze down
across our continent
all storms since you gave in, on my pup-tent.
I have of blast & counter to remercy you
for hurling me downtown.

We dream of honour, and we get along.
Fate winged me, in the person of a cab
and your stance on the sand.
Think it across, in freezing wind: withstand
my blistered wish: flop, there, to his blind song
who pick up the tab.

'Oyez, oyez!' The Man Who Did Not Deliver
is before you for his deliverance, my lords.
He stands, as charged
for This by banks, That cops, by lawyers, by
publishingers for Them. I doubt he'll make
old bones.

Be.
I warned him, of a summer night: consist,
consist. Ex-wives roar.
Further, the Crown holds that they spilt himself,
splitting his manward chances, to his shame,
my lords, & our horror.

Behind, oh worst lean backward them who bring
un-charges: hundreds & one, children,
the pillars & the sot.
Henry thought. It is so. I must sting.
Listen! the grave ground-rhythm of a gone
. . . makar? So what.

44

Tell it to the forest fire, tell it to the moon,
mention it in general to the moon
on the way down,
he's about to have his lady, permanent;
and this is the worst of all came ever sent
writhing Henry's way.

Ha ha, fifth column, quisling, genocide,
he held his hands & laught from side to side
a loverly time.
The berries & the rods left him alone less.
Thro' a race of water once I went: happiness.
I'll walk into the sky.

There the great flare & stench, O flying creatures,
surely will dim-dim? Bars will be closed.
No girl will again
conceive above your throes. A fine thunder peals
will with its friends and soon, from agony
put the fire out.

He stared at ruin. Ruin stared straight back.
He thought they was old friends. He felt on the stair
where her papa found them bare
they became familiar. When the papers were lost
rich with pals' secrets, he thought he had the knack
of ruin. Their paths crossed

and once they crossed in jail; they crossed in bed;
and over an unsigned letter their eyes met,
and in an Asian city
directionless & lurchy at two & three,
or trembling to a telephone's fresh threat,
and when some wired his head

to reach a wrong opinion, 'Epileptic'.
But he noted now that: they were not old friends.
He did not know this one.
This one was a stranger, come to make amends
for all the imposters, and to make it stick.
Henry nodded, un-.

46

I am, outside. Incredible panic rules.
People are blowing and beating each other without mercy.
Drinks are boiling. Iced
drinks are boiling. The worse anyone feels, the worse
treated he is. Fools elect fools.
A harmless man at an intersection said, under his breath: "Christ!"

That word, so spoken, affected the vision
of, when they trod to work next day, shopkeepers
who went & were fitted for glasses.
Enjoyed they then an appearance of love & law.
Millenia whift & waft—one, one—er, er . . .
Their glasses were taken from them, & they saw.

Man has undertaken the top job of all,
son fin. Good luck.
I myself walked at the funeral of tenderness.
Followed other deaths. Among the last,
like the memory of a lovely fuck,
was: *Do, ut des*.

April Fool's Day, or, St Mary of Egypt

—Thass a funny title, Mr Bones.
—When down she saw her feet, sweet fish, on the threshold,
she considered her fair shoulders
and all them hundreds who have held them, all
the more who to her mime thickened & maled
from the supple stage,

and seeing her feet, in a visit, side by side
paused on the sill of The Tomb, she shrank: 'No.
They are not worthy,
fondled by many' and rushed from The Crucified
back through her followers out of the city ho
across the suburbs, plucky

to dare my desert in her late daylight
of animals and sands. She fall prone.
Only wind whistled.
And forty-seven years went by like Einstein.
We celebrate her feast with our caps on,
whom God has not visited.

He yelled at me in Greek,
my God!—It's not his language
and I'm no good at—his is Aramaic,
was—I am a monoglot of English
(American version) and, say pieces from
a baker's dozen others: where's the bread?

but rising in the Second Gospel, pal:
The seed goes down, god dies,
a rising happens,
some crust, and then occurs   an eating. He said so,
a Greek idea,
troublesome to imaginary Jews,

like bitter Henry, full of the death of love,
Cawdor-uneasy, disambitious, mourning
the whole implausible necessary thing.
He dropped his voice & sybilled of
the death of the death of love.
I óught to get going.

49

Blind

Old Pussy-cat if he won't eat, he don't
feel good into his tum', old Pussy-cat.
He *wants* to have eaten.
Tremor, heaves, he sweaterings. He can't.
A dizzy swims of where is Henry at;
. . . somewhere streng verboten.

How come he sleeps & sleeps and sleeps, waking like death:
locate the restorations of which we hear
as of profound sleep.
From daylight he got maintrackt, from friends' breath,
wishes, his hopings. Dreams make crawl with fear
Henry but not get up.

The course his mind his body steer, poor Pussy-cat,
in weakness & disorder, will see him down
whiskers & tail.
'Wastethrift': Oh one of cunning wives know that
he hoardy-squander, where is nor downtown
neither suburba. Braille.

5 0

In a motion of night they massed nearer my post.
I hummed a short blues. When the stars went out
I studied my weapons system.
Grenades, the portable rack, the yellow spout
of the anthrax-ray: in order. Yes, and most
of my pencils were sharp.

This edge of the galaxy has often seen
a defence so stiff, but it could only go
one way.
—Mr Bones, your troubles give me vertigo,
& backache. Somehow, when I make your scene,
I cave to feel as if

de roses of dawns & pearls of dusks, made up
by some ol' writer-man, got right forgot
& the greennesses of ours.
Springwater grow so thick it gonna clot
and the pleasing ladies cease. I figure, yup,
you is bad powers.

51

Our wounds to time, from all the other times,
sea-times slow, the times of galaxies
fleeing, the dwarfs' dead times,
lessen so little that if here in his crude rimes
Henry them mentions, do not hold it, please,
for a putting of man down.

Ol' Marster, being bound you do your best
versus we coons, spare now a cagey John
a whilom bits that whip:
who'll tell your fortune, when you have confessed
whose & whose woundings—against the innocent stars
& remorseless seas—

—Are you radioactive, pal? —Pal, radioactive.
—Has you the night sweats & the day sweats, pal?
—Pal, I do.
—Did your gal leave you? —What do *you* think, pal?
—Is that thing on the front of your head what it seems to be, pal?
—Yes, pal.

52

Silent Song

Bright-eyed & bushy-tailed woke not Henry up.
Bright though upon his workshop shone a vise
central, moved in
while he was doing time down hospital
and growing wise.
He gave it the worst look he had left.

Alone. They all abandoned   Henry—wonder! all,
when most he—under the sun.
That was all right.
He can't work well with it here, or think.
A bilocation, yellow like catastrophe.
The name of this was freedom.

Will Henry again ever be on the lookout for women & milk,
honour & love again,
have a buck or three?
He felt like shrieking but he shuddered as
(spring mist, warm, rain) an handful with quietness
vanisht & the thing took hold.

5 3

He lay in the middle of the world, and twitcht.
More Sparine for Pelides,
human (half) & down here as he is,
with probably insulting mail to open
and certainly unworthy words to hear
and his unforgivable memory.

—I seldom *go* to *films*. They are too exciting,
said the Honourable Possum.
—It takes me so long to read the 'paper,
said to me one day a novelist hot as a firecracker,
because I have to identify myself with everyone in it,
including the corpses, pal.'

Kierkegaard wanted a society, to refuse to read 'papers,
and that was not, friends, his worst idea.
Tiny Hardy, toward the end, refused to say *anything*,
a programme adopted early on by long Housman,
and Gottfried Benn
said:—We are using our own skins for wallpaper and we cannot win.

5 4

'NO VISITORS' I thumb the roller to
and leans against the door.
Comfortable in my horseblanket
I prop on the costly bed & dream of my wife,
my first wife,
and my second wife & my son.

Insulting, they put guardrails up,
as if it were a crib!
I growl at the head nurse; we compose on one.
I have been operating from *nothing*,
like a dog after its tail
more slowly, losing altitude.

Nitid. They are shooting me full of sings.
I give no rules. Write as short as you can,
in order, of what matters.
I think of my beloved poet
Issa & his father who
sat down on the grass and took leave of each other.

Peter's not friendly. He gives me sideways looks.
The architecture is far from reassuring.
I feel uneasy.
A pity,—the interview began so well:
I mentioned fiendish things, he waved them away
and sloshed out a martini

strangely needed. We spoke of indifferent matters—
God's health, the vague hell of the Congo,
John's energy,
anti-matter matter. I felt fine.
Then a change came backward. A chill fell.
Talk slackened,

died, and he began to give me sideways looks.
'Christ,' I thought 'what now?' and would have askt for another
but didn't dare.
I feel my application   failing. It's growing dark,
some other sound is overcoming. His last words are:
'We betrayed me.'

5 6

Hell is empty. O that has come to pass
which the cut Alexandrian foresaw,
and Hell lies empty.
Lightning fell silent where the Devil knelt
and over the whole grave space hath settled awe
in a full death of guilt.

The tinchel closes. Terror, & plunging, swipes.
I lay my ears back. I am about to die.
My cleft feet drum.
Fierce, the two-footers club. My green world pipes
a finish—for us all, my love, not some.
Crumpling, I—why,—

So in his crystal ball them two he weighs,
solidly, dreaming of his sleepy son,
ah him, and his new wife.
What roar solved once the dilemma of the Ancient of Days,
what sigh borrowed His mercy?—Who may, if
we are all the same, make one.

5 7

In a state of chortle sin—once he reflected,
swilling tomato juice—live I, and did
more than my thirstier years.
To Hell then will it maul me? for good talk,
and gripe of retail loss? I dare say not.
I don't thínk there's that place

save sullen here, wherefrom she flies tonight
retrieving her whole body, which I need.
I recall a 'coon treed,
flashlights, & barks, and I was in that tree,
and something can (has) been said for sobriety
but very little.

The guns. Ah, darling, it was late for me,
midnight, at seven. How in famished youth
could I foresee Henry's sweet seed
unspent across so flying barren ground,
where would my loves dislimn whose dogs abound?
I fell out of the tree.

Industrious, affable, having brain on fire,
Henry perplexed himself; others gave up;
good girls gave in;
geography was hard on friendship, Sire;
marriages lashed & languished, anguished; dearth of group
and what else had been;

the splendour & the lose grew all the same,
Sire. His heart stiffened, and he failed to smile,
catching *(enfint)* on.
The law: we must, owing to chiefly shame
lacing our pride, down what we did. A mile,
a mile to Avalon.

Stuffy & lazy, shaky, making roar
overseas presses, he quit wondering:
the mystery is full.
Sire, damp me down. Me feudal O, me yore
(male Muse) serf, if anyfing;
which rank I pull.

Henry's Meditation in the Kremlin

Down on the cathedrals, as from the Giralda
in a land no crueller, and over the walls
to domes & river look
from Great John's belfry, Ivan-Veliky,
whose thirty-one are still
to hail who storms no father's throne. Bell, book

& candle rule, in silence. Hour by hour
from time to time with holy oil
touch yet the forehead eyelids nose
lips ears breast fists of Krushchev, for Christ knows
poor evil Kadar, cut, is back in power.
Boils his throne. The moujik kneels & votes.

South & east of the others' tombs—where? why,
in Arkhanghelsky, on the Baptist's side,
lies Brother Jonas (formerly Ivan the Terrible),
where Brother Josef came with his fiend's heart
out of such guilt it proved all bearable,
and Brother Nikita will come and lie.

60

Afters eight years, be less dan eight percent,
distinguish' friend, of coloured wif de whites
in de School, in de Souf.
—Is coloured gobs, is coloured officers,
Mr Bones. Dat's nuffin? —Uncle Tom,
sweep shut yo mouf,

is million blocking from de proper job,
de fairest houses & de churches eben.
—You may be right, Friend Bones.
Indeed you is. Dey flyin ober de world,
de pilots, ober ofays. Bit by bit
our immemorial moans

brown down to all dere moans. I flees that, sah.
They brownin up to ourn. Who gonna win?
—I wouldn't *pre*dict.
But I do guess mos peoples gonna *lose*.
I never saw no pinkie wifout no hand.
O my, without no hand.

6 1

Full moon. Our Narragansett gales subside
and the land is celebrating men of war
more or less, less or more.
In valleys, thin on headlands, narrow & wide
our targets rest. In us we trust. Far, near,
the bivouacs of fear

are solemn in the moon somewhere tonight,
in turning time. It's late for gratitude,
an annual, rude
roar of a moment's turkey's 'Thanks'. Bright & white
their ordered markers undulate away
awaiting no day.

Away from us, from Henry's feel or fail,
campaigners lie with mouldered toes, disarmed,
out of order,
with whom we will one. The war is real,
and a sullen glory pauses over them harmed,
incident to murder.

6 2

That dark brown rabbit, lightness in his ears
& underneath, gladdened our afternoon
munching a crab-'.
That rabbit was a fraud, like a black bull
prudent I admired in Zaragoza, who
certainly was brave as a demon

but would not charge, being willing not to die.
The rabbit's case, a little different,
consisted in alert
& wily looks down the lawn, where nobody was,
with prickt ears, while rapt but chatting on the porch
we sat in view nearby.

Then went he mildly by, and around behind
my cabin, and when I followed, there he just sat.
Only at last
he turned down around, passing my wife at four feet
and hopped the whole lawn and made thro' the hedge for the big
    house.
—Mr Bones, we all brutes & fools.

Bats have no bankers and they do not drink
and cannot be arrested and pay no tax
and, in general, bats have it made.
Henry for joining the human race is *bats*,
known to be so, by few them who think,
out of the cave.

Instead of the cave! ah lovely-chilly, dark,
ur-moist his cousins hang in hundreds or swerve
with personal radar,
crisisless, kid. Instead of the cave? I serve,
inside, my blind term. Filthy four-foot lights
reflect on the whites of our eyes.

He then salutes for sixty years of it
just now a one of valor and insights,
a theatrical man,
O scholar & Legionnaire who as quickly might
have killed as cast you. *Olè*. Stormed with years
he tranquil commands and appears.

Supreme my holdings, greater yet my need,
thoughtless I go out.   Dawn.   Have I my cig's,
my flaskie O,
O crystal cock,—my kneel has gone to seed,—
and anybody's blessing? (Blast the MIGs
for making fumble so

my tardy readying.) Yes, utter' that.
Anybody's blessing? —Mr Bones,
you makes too much
démand. I might be 'fording you a hat:
it gonna rain. —I knew a one of groans
& greed & spite, of a crutch,

who thought he had, a vile night, been—well—blest.
He see someone run off. Why not Henry,
with his grasp of desire?
—Hear matters hard to manage at de best,
Mr Bones. Tween what we see, what be,
is blinds. Them blinds' on fire.

A freaking ankle crabbed his blissful trips,
this whisky tastes like California
but is Kentucky,
like Berkeley where he truly worked at it
but nothing broke all night—no fires—one dawn,
crowding his luck,

flowed down along the cliffs to the Big Sur
where Henry Miller's box is vomit-green
and Henry bathed in sulphur
lovely, hot, over the sea, like Senator
Cat, relaxed & sober, watery
as Tivoli, sir.

No Christmas jaunts for fractured cats. Hot dog,
the world is places where he will not go
this wintertide or again.
Does Striding Edge block wild the sky as then
when Henry with his mystery was two
& twenty, high on the hog?

66

'All virtues enter into this world:')
A Buddhist, doused in the street, serenely burned.
The Secretary of State for War,
winking it over, screwed a redhaired whore.
Monsignor Capovilla mourned. What a week.
A journalism doggy took a leak

against absconding coon ('but take one virtue,
without which a man can hardly hold his own')
the sun in the willow
shivers itself & shakes itself green-yellow
(Abba Pimen groaned, over the telephone,
when asked what that was:)

How feel a fellow then when he arrive
in fame but lost? but affable, top-shelf.
Quelle sad semaine.
He hardly know his selving. ('that a man')
Henry grew hot, got laid, felt bad, survived
('should always reproach himself'.

I don't operate often. When I do,
persons take note.
Nurses look amazed. They pale.
The patient is brought back to life, or so.
The reason I don't do this more (I quote)
is: I have a living to fail—

because of my wife & son—to keep from earning.
—Mr Bones, I sees that.
They for these operations thanks you, what?
not pays you. —Right.
You have seldom been so understanding.
Now there is further a difficulty with the light:

I am obliged to perform in complete darkness
operations of great delicacy
on my self.
—Mr Bones, you terrifies me.
No wonder they don't pay you. Will you die?
—My
               friend, I succeeded. Later.

6 8

I heard, could be, a Hey there from the wing,
and I went on: Miss Bessie soundin good
that one, that night of all,
I feelin fair mysef, taxes & things
seem to be back in line, like everybody should
and nobody in the snow on call

so, as I say, the house is givin hell
to *Yellow Dog,* I blowin like it too
and Bessie always do
when she make a very big sound—after, well,
no sound—I see she totterin—I cross which stage
even at Henry's age

in 2-3 seconds: then we wait and see.
I hear strange horns, Pinetop he hit some chords,
Charlie start *Empty Bed,*
they all come hangin Christmas on some tree
after trees thrown out—sick-house's white birds',
black to the birds instead.

Love her he doesn't but the thought he puts
into that young woman
would launch a national product
complete with TV spots & skywriting
outlets in Bonn & Tokyo
I mean it

Let it be known that nine words have not passed
between herself and Henry;
looks, smiles.
God help Henry, who deserves it all
every least part of that infernal & unconscious
woman, and the pain.

I feel as if, unique, she . . . Biddable?
Fates, conspire.
—Mr Bones, *please*.
—Vouchsafe me, Sleepless One,
a personal experience of the body of Mrs Boogry
before I pass from lust!

Disengaged, bloody, Henry rose from the shell
where in their racing start his seat got wedged
under his knifing knees,
he did it on the runners, feathering,
being bow, catching no crab. The ridges were sore
& tore chamois. It was not done with ease.

So Henry was a hero, malgré lui,
that day, for blundering; until & after the coach
said this & which to him.
That happy day, whenas the pregnant back
of Number Two returned, and he'd no choice
but to make for it room.

Therefore he rowed rowed rowed. They did not win.
Forever in the winning & losing since
of his own crew, or rather
in the weird regattas of this afterworld,
cheer for the foe. He set himself to time
the blue father.

Spellbound held subtle Henry all his four
hearers in the racket of the market
with ancient signs, infamous characters,
new rhythms. On the steps he was beloved,
hours a day, by all his four, or more,
depending. And they paid him.

It was not, so, like no one listening
but critics famed & Henry's pals or other
tellers at all
chiefly in another country. No.
He by the heart & brains & tail, because
of their love for it, had them.

Junk he said to all them open-mouthed.
Weather wóuld govern. When the monsoon spread
its floods, few came, two.
Came a day when none, though he began
in his accustomed way on the filthy steps
in a crash of waters, came.

7 2

The Elder Presences

Shh! on a twine hung from disastered trees
Henry is swinging his daughter. They seem drunk.
Over across them look out,
tranquil, the high statues of the wise.
Her feet peep, like a lady's in sleep sunk.
That which this scene's about—

he pushes violent, his calves distend,
his mouth is open with effort, so is hers,
in the Supreme Court garden,
the justices lean, negro, out, the trees bend,
man's try began too long ago, with chirrs
& leapings, begging pardon—

I will deny the gods of the garden say.
Henry's perhaps to break his burnt-cork luck.
I further will deny
good got us up that broad shoreline. Greed may
like a fuse, but with the high shore we is stuck,
whom they overlook. Why,—

7 3

Karesansui, Ryoan-ji

The taxi makes the vegetables fly.
'Dozo kudasai,' I have him wait.
Past the bright lake up into the temple,
shoes off, and
my right leg swings me left.
I do survive beside the garden I

came seven thousand mile the other way
supplied of engines all to see, to see.
Differ them photographs, plans lie:
how big it is!
austere a sea rectangular   of sand by the oiled mud wall,
and the sand is not quite white: granite sand, grey,

—from nowhere can one see *all* the stones—
but helicopters or   a Brooklyn reproduction
will fix that—

and the fifteen changeless stones in their five worlds
with a shelving of moving moss
stand me the thought of the ancient maker priest.
Elsewhere occurs—I remembers—loss.
Through awes & weathers neither it increased
nor did one blow of all his stone & sand thought die.

7 4

Henry hates the world. What the world to Henry
did will not bear thought.
Feeling no pain,
Henry stabbed his arm and wrote a letter
explaining how bad it had been
in this world.

Old yellow, in a gown
might have made a difference, 'these lower beauties',
and chartreuse could have mattered

"Kyoto, Toledo,
Benares—the holy cities—
and Cambridge shimmering do not make up
for, well, the horror of unlove,
nor south from Paris driving in the Spring
to Siena and on . . ."

Pulling together Henry, somber Henry
woofed at things.
Spry disappointments of men
and vicing adorable children
miserable women, Henry mastered, Henry
tasting all the secret bits of life.

75

Turning it over, considering, like a madman
Henry put forth a book.
No harm resulted from this.
Neither the menstruating   stars (nor man) was moved
at once.
Bare dogs drew closer for a second look

and performed their friendly operations there.
Refreshed, the bark rejoiced.
Seasons went and came.
Leaves fell, but only a few.
Something remarkable about this
unshedding bulky bole-proud blue-green moist

thing made by savage & thoughtful
surviving Henry
began to strike the passers from despair
so that sore on their shoulders old men hoisted
six-foot sons and polished women called
small girls to dream awhile toward the flashing & bursting
    tree!

76

Henry's Confession

Nothin very bad happen to me lately.
How you explain that? —I explain that, Mr Bones,
terms o' your bafflin odd sobriety.
Sober as man can get, no girls, no telephones,
what could happen bad to Mr Bones?
—*If* life is a handkerchief sandwich,

in a modesty of death I join my father
who dared so long agone leave me.
A bullet on a concrete stoop
close by a smothering southern sea
spreadeagled on an island, by my knee.
—You is from hunger, Mr Bones,

I offers you this handkerchief, now set
your left foot by my right foot,
shoulder to shoulder, all that jazz,
arm in arm, by the beautiful sea,
hum a little, Mr Bones.
—I saw nobody coming, so I went instead.

Seedy Henry rose up shy in de world
& shaved & swung his barbells, duded Henry up
and p.a.'d poor thousands of persons on topics of grand
moment to Henry, ah to those less & none.
Wif a book of his in either hand
he is stript down to move on.

—Come away, Mr Bones.

—Henry is tired of the winter,
& haircuts, & a squeamish comfy   ruin-prone proud national
    mind,   & Spring (in the city so called).
Henry likes Fall.
Hé would be prepared to líve in a world of Fáll
for ever, impenitent Henry.
But the snows and summers grieve & dream;

thése fierce & airy occupations, and love,
raved away so many of Henry's years
it is a wonder that, with in each hand
one of his own mad books and all,
ancient fires for eyes, his head full
& his heart full, he's making ready to move on.

Printed in the USA
CPSIA information can be obtained
at www.ICGtesting.com
LVHW010341150724
785510LV00002B/214